Water Chemistry 101 for your Swimming Pool
Pro Pool Girl

All Rights Reserved. No part of this publication may be reproduced in any form or by any means, including scanning, photocopying, or otherwise without prior written permission of the copyright holder. Copyright © 2013

Table of Contents

1. Testing Your Swimming Pool Water
2. The Basics and Must Haves to Balance Water
3. Help It Party Time and My Pool Is Green
4. What Does My Filter Have To Do With My Water
5. A Word about Phosphates

1. Testing Your Swimming Pool Water

Keeping your swimming pool water in balance chemically is an important part of pool ownership. Proper maintenance can prevent damage to equipment, eliminate and keep at bay parasites and germs which can cause rashes, prevent burning eyes and other illness as well keep a group of kids happily swimming versus sitting on the sidelines because the water is cloudy and green. No one wants to swim in a nasty pool; the goal is to have sparkling clear, sanitized water.

Your water should be tested regularly and adjusted to meet the proper required levels. I often get asked how often you should test your water and my answer is as often as you would like but a minimum of 2-3 times a week. Your water's chemical balance is constantly changing and everything from weather to oils and sweat from bathers, to dirt and cosmetics can affect it. Any time you notice a change in your water quality get your test kit out or bring it up to your local pool store for testing.

Let's just talk weather for a minute; since I am from the Northeast our weather can have a big effect on swimming pool water. Rain can be acidic and winds can drop all sorts of things down into the pool water including particles of molds, pollens, and other air born materials which can cause havoc with your pool. So my suggestion would be after a rain storm or high winds immediately skim the top of the pool and remove fallen leaves and whatever else fell in there and test your pool water. In our area for example; rain tends to lower PH Levels and Alkaline Levels. For pools in the Southeast and West weather will also affect your pool water chemistry. The warmer sunny climates obviously allow owners to use their pools for a longer swimming season and for many year round. In these climates weather issues such as strong sun, extreme heat and lack of rain can cause quicker use of chemicals such as chlorine. More volatile winds as an example in coastal areas can place more organic particles in the pool and of course evaporation which means you are adding water often to the pool and therefore need to re-balance your pools chemistry often and diligently as the hotter it gets the more quickly the pool can change to a swamp pool. Good for gators, not so good for swimmers.

There are several methods to use in testing swimming pool water some easier than others and some more accurate than others. We want of course to take the simplest method which I think is the strip method. These strips can test for levels of total Chlorine, Free Chlorine, PH, Alkaline, Hardness, and Cyanuric Acid (Six Way) or just the three main tests of Total Chlorine, PH, and Alkaline (Three Way). For residential pools these are going to be the main components you will look at. The strips are easy, immerse the strip and swirl 3 times in a one foot circle and then raise strip from water face up and keep level to avoid reactant on strip pads from running. Compare your results starting with the end pad starting with the free chlorine and end with the total hardness pad, this allows for the correct reaction time for the different pads.

The pros of these strips is the ease in which you test, the cons are that once you compare colors of the pads it will not give you an exact amount of correlating chemicals necessary to bring the water up to the proper level. I also find that if you have too much chlorine in the pool the pad for chlorine readings will bleach out leaving no color to compare and the tester thinking there is no chlorine in the pool when in fact there may be too much.

Drop Test?
Another method to test the pool water is by using a liquid reagent test kit. These kits, also simple to use usually include two small bottles of reagents one testing Total Chlorine and the other PH. There is usually a small container that has two sides that hold two separate samples of water. When taking a sample make sure you are taking a proper sample up to the fill line on the container, add drops holding the dropper bottle vertically (straight up and down) as holding at an angle may distort the drop size and lead to inaccurate results, and always wash out the container after each test. The plastic test tube on each side has a color comparison chart which will tell you if you have no level, low or too high. The pros of the liquid

drops are that it is also easy to use, and if you are testing for just Chlorine and PH it usually will be more accurate. If however you want to test for the other water levels the drop test can seem complicated and elaborate. Other negatives are that if you test for the six recommended chemicals it can be tedious and time consuming and like the strips does not tell you the amount of chemical needed to fix the level. The reagents should not be handled carelessly as some of them are toxic and if they get on your skin wash them off immediately. For a residential pool either method is fine, my preference is the strips or as I tell my customers bring a sample to your local pool professional and they can recommend the proper levels and dosage in more detail according to your region, and pool specifics.

$$$TIP: If you are having a problem with your pool water that regular testing and dosage is not correcting, bring a test sample of water to a reputable professional where they can test with a computer that will give you more *clarity* (no pun intended) as to dosage. They should ask you questions as to your what is your pool size, whether you have a lot of trees, how long you run your filter, what you have in inventory at home and test further for phosphates and nitrates if they feel it is necessary. We are in the business to serve the customer and sell chemicals but at no point should you be spending hundreds of dollars on chemicals off one test. If the pool water is that bad, fix the Chlorine, Alkaline and PH levels first, Algaecide if you have visible algae but fix these first and retest after a few days. Ask questions, if you get a funny feeling the tester doesn't know what they are talking about go somewhere with experienced people (they likely won't be a chemist but they should have knowledge about chemistry and their product) it can save you hundreds of dollars over the entire season.

The Recommended Levels:	Min	Ideal	Max
Free Chlorine (ppm)	1.0	1.0-3.0	5.0
PH	7.2	7.4-7.6	7.8
Total Alkaline	60	80-120	180
Calcium Hardness	150	200-300	400
Cyanuric Acid	10	30-50	100

Gunite or Plaster Pools maximum alkalinity should only be kept at apx. 120 while at the same time Hardness levels should be higher than liner pools Apx. 250-300

$$TIP: When adding any chemical and you are unsure of your pools volume add chemicals in small increments, it is better to add a little and retest than to add too much and have to purchase a chemical to bring your mistake back down.

It is important to know your pools volume in gallons prior to adding chemicals. It is also key to have proper expectations; if your pool looks like a swamp there is no chemical to make it clean and clear in an hour, you must be able to allow your water to filter and it may take 24-48 hours before you see results depending on the filter, it's size and amount of time you run your filter.

TIP: To calculate your pools volume:

Rectangular Shape: multiply Length x Width x Average Depth x 7.48 = Volume in Gallons Average Depth= Shallow End Depth + Deep End Depth/2=AD

Ex: 16x32 Rectangle 3ft shallow 8ft deep end

16 x 32 x (3+8=11/2)5.5x7.48=21064 Gallons

Round Shape you multiply Depth x Diameter Squared x 5.9 = Volume in Gallons ex: 24 Round Pool, 4ft deep

4x24x24x5.9=13594 Gallons

Further calculations can be used for free form pools and other designs with measurements taken at various changes to the pool shape and depths. There are several websites available now that will calculate the volume in gallons for you when you plug in these measurements. Your pool store will also be able to calculate the gallons in your pool with the proper measurements you provide.

2. The Basics and Must Haves to Balance Water

So what are the basics to water chemistry? Let's start at the beginning when you open the pool for the season and start up your filter system. I usually advise to add enough shock for your size pool and if you have algae from the winter season on the bottom to add a dosage of algaecide first and run the filter 24-48 hours. Once the water is clearing and you have completed a vacuuming picking up the big stuff, test the pool water for the common chemicals needed to balance the pool.

The most common areas to pay attention to in water chemistry to initially balance your pool water are Chlorination, Alkaline and PH. Low Alkalinity makes it more difficult to control your PH level so raise your alkaline first, retest and then do the PH level. Lack off or high levels of Alkaline and PH can lead to corrosive water environment and may damage your pool equipment and pool surfaces. Heaters are especially susceptible, in particular the heat exchangers which of course are the most expensive part to replace so beware and keep your levels correct as bad water chemistry is not a reason covered under a manufacturer's warranty. Both high and low alkalinity can cause cloudy water and make it difficult to balance the rest of your pool. If it is necessary to add both Alkaline and PH increaser, add the Alkaline first wait a few hours before adding the PH.

Low Chlorine levels can easily cause cloudiness as well, there are two types of chlorine, free and total. I usually explain the free as what is available to work but is sitting on its laurels so to speak. Shocking the pool will usually get these to work fast and clear up the cloudiness should everything else show balanced. I always suggest using liquid chlorine shock over a powder, because there is no residue sitting on your liner, just walk around the pool perimeter and put the gallon in. This is in addition to what you are using as your regular chlorination program be it Trichlor, Dichlor (powder), salt, etc. Different kinds of chlorine can lower or raise your PH levels so try to test water regularly; for example: Super Shock can raise PH levels while Trichlor can lower PH (tricky isn't it) but put simply, if your pool is cloudy check for Chlorine, PH and Alkaline levels first, bet you one or two are off and need rebalancing.

CAUTION: Add chemicals according to the label and one at time never mix together. If chemical spills on your skin wash it off immediately.

Here are some trouble shooting issues you may come across:

- *Can't keep chlorine in pool-* make sure water is balanced, add Stabilizer (Cyanuric Acid Level Low) this helps sunlight's UV's from drawing chlorine from pool
- *Pool has green particles on bottom or visible algae, bottom of pool is slippery/slimy-*there are several forms of Algae, Green, Mustard/Yellow, Black and Coral just to name a few. Green algae tend to be the easiest to treat with an algaecide, Black and Mustard algae are somewhat resistant to chlorine so get an Algaecide specific to the kind you have. Black Algae for a vinyl liner pool can be extremely difficult to deal with, you may never really get rid of it but you may be able to keep it faded with higher chlorine levels and treatments of a Black Algaecide. Black Algae has a hard coating or shell on top of it, by taking a wire brush and breaking the coating algaecide can kill the algae. This is easier with gunite pools as wire brushes cannot be used on vinyl surfaces. In our geographic area Black Algae can also be confused with Black Mold.
- *Rusty reddish yellow stains-* may be sign of metals in your water. If you fill your pool with well water or had a ton of leaves deteriorate in the bottom of the pool over the winter or your chemistry is off and your equipment such as a heat exchanger may be leaking metals into the pool water. If this is the case use a metal remover and follow instructions

carefully. A particular stains color will usually indicate what metal is in the pool; **Iron**- usually brownish red, **Copper**- blue green (can also be a sign of a bad heat exchanger), **Manganese**- pink red black or brownish black stain.

TIP: If you add a shock product to your water and the pool water turns an instant green/lime green color test for metals. If the color of your water is lime green tint but shows no signs of algae and all your other levels are good test for metals.

TIP: After doing a metal out treatment always clean your filter system thoroughly. Backwash or take cartridge out and clean well so metals do not go back in pool.

If you have done everything chemically to fix a water problem with minimal results then the issue may lie with your filtration system, here are some helpful hints based on filter type:

- Sand Filter-If you find that the filter pressure is not building up check your sand, replace if more than three years old or the particles may be too small where the sand may need help picking them up. You can try a flocculent product which drops particles to the bottom for vacuuming or a clarifier that will enlarge the particles so filter will pick them up. If the filter pressure is too high it will not be filtering very efficiently so try to backwash to bring the pressure down to a normal level.

- DE Filter-Backwash, if pressure is too high, you will notice that there is little to no water flow back into the pool so backwash and **recharge** with new earth.

- Cartridge Filters-Take out the cartridge and clean it well. Especially if you had a bad algae bloom.

- Above-Ground pools-The skimmer and single returns are the only way water is getting moved back into the pool. If the top foot of water in your pool is clear but the rest is cloudy or milky you may have poor circulation, try pointing your return eyeball (s) down to get water moving at a lower level. You can also attach your manual vacuum and put it at the bottom of the pool with the vacuum head tilted on its side to suction more water from the bottom. You can also try a clarifier.

- Vinyl In-Ground-if you are cloudy only in the deeper end of the pool again circulation may be the issue and you should point your returns downward to get the water moving or try the vacuum head tilted on the side drawing the water up and circulating through the filter system. You can also try to get your returns to form a whirlpool effect to increase circulation. If you have a Main Drain make sure it is clear of leaves and materials. Check filter for pressure reading and test water.

- Check for Phosphates! If you seem to retain your chlorine levels then check for phosphates and treat accordingly.

TIP: I want to throw a caution out there about clarifiers. Follow the dosage on the label, if you overdose (the whole bottle) you can clog your filter system and find a need to clean or backwash your system wasting both water and chemicals. I know it's tempting to throw the whole bottle in thinking it can only work faster but you are not going to win.

SOME CHEMICAL SAFETY TIPS!

1. Keep out of children and pets reach
2. Never mix chemicals together. Add separately and slowly. Never add water to chemicals, add chemicals to water.
3. Don't smoke around chemicals!
4. Always store chemical products in a cool, dry well-ventilated area.
5. Don't inhale fumes or let chemicals come into contact with eyes, nose or mouth.

In case of contact or swallowed, follow emergency advice on product label and call local poison control center and doctor.

6. Keep chemical containers closed when not in use.

7. Never tamper with labels or switch chemical out of its original container.

8. Use exact quantities specified, not more. Chemicals need to circulate for hours before retesting water.

9. Less is more don't stock up on chemicals. Shelf life is important so dispose of according to the hazardous waste disposal rules of your community.

10. If a spill occurs follow clean up instructions per label or call local emergency # and keep spilled item isolated.

I hope this helps a little in your swimming pool endeavors. Try not to add too much chemical to your pool as this is not environmentally friendly and eventually adds up to Total Dissolved Solids which I didn't even cover here (TDS) just remember you are swimming in this pool. If in doubt bring a sample to a pool store where they don't push a bunch of chemical on you but sell you what you need.

It is important to remember that your pool equipment will make a difference as to the time it takes to clear up a pool and filter chemicals as an example: a sand filter usually takes longer than a DE filter because a DE filter can pick up particles 2-5 microns in size where a sand filter will filter particles in size of 50-100 microns.

I am listing some chemicals that are quite common for use and what their functions are for a brief overview, but remember the pool professional or the product label can be an invaluable source on what your particular pool water needs:

Balancers: The chemicals such as PH Increase and PH Decrease, Alkaline Increaser, Stabilizer and Calcium Hardness Increaser or Decrease.

Total alkalinity is the ability of water to resist changes in PH or put simply the ability to keep water from wide pH swings. Total alkalinity helps protect your equipment, pool surfaces, maximizes sanitizer efficiency and makes the water more comfortable. Having low alkalinity makes it hard to control the pH which can lead to corrosive water and damage your pool equipment. High alkalinity can cause cloudiness of your water.

Calcium Hardness is the measure of dissolved calcium minerals in your water. A low level of
Calcium Hardness will tend to be aggressive, causing equipment corrosion and etching in plaster and masonry pools. Water with high levels of calcium hardness typically have cloudy water and mineral deposits and is called scaling.

Cyanuric Acid (Stabilizer) Stabilizer conditions pool water to prevent chlorine loss due to sunlight. It is very important in Salt pools and can be a cost saver if you find you are using too much chlorine. You will usually put in the pool 2-3 times a season.

Sanitizers: Tricolor in 3inch or 1inch tabs. These will usually be of quality and concentration of around 98-99% Trichlor and possess some stabilizer in the tab as well.

Granular Dichlor-is usually 56% available chlorine and the rest is fillers, there is no stabilizer built in and you should run the filter twelve hours after application.

Bromine: Bromine can come in powder, tab or flake form. It does not give up a harsh odor according to the label and may be less harsh on skin. Bromine will not be the most cost effective way to maintain your pool water. Lithium is also available for those allergic or sensitive to chlorine, again not a cheap form of sanitizing.

In addition to chemical sanitizers there are also mechanical forms to assist with sanitizing for your pool such as Ozone and UV producers. Both of these still will need balancing chemicals and some form of chlorine but will help lower the amount you will need to use.

Other chlorine producers that have become quite popular are Salt Systems and other mineral systems. All of these Sanitizer options should be discussed and planned so that you understand the maintenance and care of each.

Algaecide's: These come in several forms and strengths. There are copper based, and polyquats; black, green, red or coral and mustard algaecide. Select the one that will fit what you are experiencing. For maintenance, I usually suggest a Poly 60 (especially for salt pools) which usually is a few ounces weekly to prevent algae so long as you maintain your pool water at the proper levels.

The main types of algae are:

- *Green Algae* – usually floating algae, but sometimes clings to walls. Prior to seeing the green particles you may notice the sides of the pool having a slippery feel, your water may become cloudy and you may have an issue keeping chlorine levels at the appropriate levels.
- *Mustard (Yellow) Algae* – shows itself as a yellow powdery deposit on the pool, you will see yellow algae in shady areas of your pool Once established, it is chlorine-resistant and can exist in the presence of 3-5 ppm Free Chlorine.
- *Black (Blue-Green) Algae* – known by the formation of dime to quarter-size black (or blue-green) spots, these algae adheres to the pool surface. It is very difficult to remove once it begins. Black algae forms a layered structure where the first layers, might be killed by chlorine, but the under layers, like mustard algae, is also chlorine-resistant.
- *Coral or Red Algae*- Manifests itself by attaching to your pools plastic return covers, skimmers, stairs initially. I have had success removing this algae by using a silver algaecide.

Metal & Scale: These chemicals would include Calcium Reducers, Metal Sequesters and and Stain Removers. Many of these will require your chlorine levels to be in range, some will need PH levels to be a little higher than normal and many require backwashing or cleaning your filter at different time intervals so read every label carefully. For well owners, the process of backwashing can become a vicious cycle as you will need to top off the pool after a metal treatment once again introducing metals into the pool. Try to find metal removers that do not require as many backwash sessions and use a maintenance product afterward.

Problem Solvers: These chemical products would include your Clarifier's, Phosphate Removers, Flocks, Filter Cleaners and Enzyme Refreshers. There are many more out there but I would use caution as to how much you throw into your pool, they will chemically alter the water and may change the balance of your other levels. The most popular in our area is the Clarifier. However as I mentioned in my blog www.prospectpoolsllc.com/blog too much Clarifier can clog some filter systems, as do Flocculants. Many of these problem solvers require you to wash out your cartridge or backwash your DE and Sand Filters.

Shock Products: Many think a shock is a shock is a shock. Not so. There are several variations and forms to shock your pool with. My preference is liquid shock. One gallon per 10000gal of pool water is the usual dosage and you can just walk around the perimeter of the pool and distribute evenly or pour in a bucket of pool water then walk around and pour. I like this over powder shock because the powder even if you dilute in a bucket of water can still have undiluted particles that can sit on the bottom of your pool and diminish the strength and color of your pool liner and surface. There is also non-chlorine shock which is effective when your pool has chloramines (a strong chlorine odor and cloudy water is a hint that you may need a non-chlorine shock product). Some believe you should shock the pool once a week, I am of the school that this method is not necessary unless testing calls for a treatment. The need for shock treatment will depend on several factors including water test, bather load, weather etc. If it's just you going in the pool once in a while and everything tests out fine you don't need to shock in my opinion, whereas I would likely shock after pool!

3. Help Its Party Time and My Pool Is Green

Well, the big party weekend is upon us and for those who have been too busy to open your swimming pool yet or have been procrastinating due to the unseasonably cool weather are now raising your heads and thinking hmmm we could have a party, nice weather coming and yet your pool may open looking like something of a different sort partied there all winter.

There is no magic pill that is going to get you out of the mess only proper chemical balance and elbow grease but here are some ideas. By the way if your party is in an hour you better have some good food and drink and just enjoy the day as it is not likely you will be swimming no matter how many chemicals you put in there. If you are opening the pool this weekend and it opens clear fantastic, get your filter running, start your chlorination and balance your water and you are good to go for a swim. Use a non-chlorine shock if you are swimming immediately, if you are using a chlorine shock wait 2 hours before going into pool. If your pool has a slight haze to it and everything else is in balance the shock treatment should bring you back to sparkling blue.

Now if you are the procrastinator and your pool has an algae party going on you will need to call the algae cops to boot them out with an algaecide letting your filter run continuously for 12-24hrs and then vacuum one or two times till clear. Again balance your water and get your chlorine going ASAP! Now if everything seems to be happening except that your pool just isn't crystal clear but all your chemical levels seem on the money, you can try some clarifier which makes the tiny particles that the filter isn't picking up bigger so that it can. Clarifier can actually work fairly quickly, *no your swamp won't be blue in an hour* but I have had a cloudy pool turn clear in a few hours, it will all depend on the size of your pool and size and type of your filter. For the best results bring your water up to a reputable pool store that tests water and start there first rather than trying to guess, remember you don't want to throw in unnecessary chemicals as this will add to TDS (total dissolved solids) in your water and may come up to bite you in the butt later with a more severe water problem. Follow a professionals' instructions or read the label and add the proper dosage.

Be careful not to do foolish things under the pressure of one party! You have the entire summer to rock on! Don't empty your pool if you have a vinyl liner as this may cause shrinkage (no not that kind) and you may not be able to fill it up again (new liner! Big bucks!) yes this seems like an easy way out by adding all new water but your short cut can be an expensive mistake. If the algaecide label says 4-5 oz. per 10,000 gallons don't throw the entire bottle in there, it won't hurt but some algaecide s will foam and you'll feel like your swimming in a bubble bath not a pool. If this does happen the suds will dissipate with time, chlorine and sunshine.

Don't cut corners on safety issues either. Remember parties = children and have a designated supervisor at the pool at all times children are in the pool. Don't drink and drive? DON'T DRINK AND DIVE!!!! Keep the fun at a high level and party on safely.

4. What Does My Filter Have To Do With My Water

After being in this business for years, I am always amazed at the naivety of customers when it comes to their pool equipment. In the past few years I have had people come in and explain that their pool water is always cloudy or green and they don't understand why. When I begin asking questions on what type of chemicals they have put in so far, do they have a heater and what temp do they keep it at, as well as the type of filter and pump they have they either have no problem answering or they don't know or they lie. Yes people do lie for some reason. Last year, I had a couple come in the store quite frequently and whenever I asked them how long they are running their filter system for the answer was always "all the time". Finally towards the tail end of the season I asked the question again they finally told me they run the filter for an hour a day. Really! There's the answer, you can't expect to have clear, clean, sanitized water when you are running the pump and filter an hour a day.

There are so many cool innovations on the market today that can eliminate the fear that you will be relinquishing your paycheck to the electric company by running the filter 8-10 hours a day. You have to remember that a filter system cycles so many gallons of water per minute. For example a system may cycle 19000 gals every 8 hours, so if you have a 16x32 rectangle pool that has 21000 gallons, you need to run the filter for 8-10 hours to filter that pool just one time. If you had another type of system you could filter 48000 gallons every 8 hours.

Filter selection as in proper size and pump horse power as well as operating the system for a period of time to filter at least once preferably twice the volume of your pool in an 8 hour period. Today's technology allows you to run your system with such efficiency that I will often suggest longer periods of filtering when we are entering into heat waves and weather events causing organic and natural particles to be more present during certain times of the year. I personally, run my filter 24/7 at times. For me, I have minimal amount of time to vacuum and clean the pool and find if I leave the pump on I rarely have to do any maintenance except for testing my water and skimming the top of pool once a week.
You may think that I am being wasteful of energy using my system this way, but I have a variable speed pump which because of technology I can program to run at various speeds depending upon weather, how much use the pool is getting and my surrounding environment. The systems out today are extremely energy sufficient and are built to adapt to variable circumstances of each individual. An example: someone who has their pool located in full sun will have to keep a more diligent eye on their chlorine levels as the sun will pull the chlorine out more quickly than if the pool was mostly shaded, or if a pool is in a more wooded area it may have more

organic material such as pollens, leaves, needles etc. that will need to be filtered.

Also a consideration is if you have some sort of automated chlorination system such as a chlorinator, salt or mineral system and some other type of UV or Ozonators, you have to remember that the filter needs to be running to produce and introduce the chlorine into your pool water.

$TIP: By adding Stabilizer 2-3 times a year you can enhance the stability of chlorine in your pool by holding the chlorine a little longer in the pool by protecting against the suns UV rays from drawing it out.

So what type of filter systems are out there? There are three main types of filters out there for sale in the main stream pool world.

- Diatomaceous Earth or (DE) as it's called is a filter system which may contain elements either known as "fingers" or "grids" which get coated with the DE. The water then is pulled into the pump and goes through the filter tank where the dirty and contaminated particles are pick up by the DE. It is the most efficient filter system as far as the size of particles it will pick up measured in microns. The DE filters can filter particles as small as 1-4 microns.

- Cartridge filters usually have one or more pleated cartridges (look like an air filer) and can pick up particles 10 microns and up.

- Sand Filters maintain your pool by having sand filter out dirt and contaminants. Of the three I find it to be the least efficient as it filters particles as small as 40 microns which means some of the smaller contaminants will bypass and go right back into your pool water.

Again the innovation of other types of filter media such as various forms of DE and pea gravel and glass are showing some promise at improving filter capacity but at this juncture they have not proved to be very economical to make a change just yet. For our area, we sell many DE filters because of their efficiency and cleaning power. You can clean a normal size pool in a day where it may take 2-3 for a Sand filter.

The sizing of your filter will also have an effect as to how long it will take to filter your pools volume of water. Most will give an explanation as to how many square feet the filter size is designed for. It's important to take into consideration, your pools size and volume in gallons as well as your pumps horsepower, and your plumbing size, is it 1 1/2, 2 and even 3 inch piping? If you have questions call your pool guy or girl.

As far as pool pumps go, sizing is also important. There are so many various sizes out there from ¾ horsepower and up. If you have an in the ground pool with a two return lines and one skimmer you will be fine with a 1hp pump, but if you have a pool that is running waterfalls, ponds, fountains or other water features you will want to either go higher in horsepower or have more than one pump. As I mentioned earlier, the variable and two speed pumps can be very efficient and programmed according to your outside environment and lifestyle. California now requires these types of pumps to be put on all new installations for energy conservation, as California goes so do others and eventually the old style pumps will be discontinued.

$$TIP: Currently the variable speed and two speed pumps will cost you more initial outlay when installing, however when programmed correctly your energy savings can be 50-60% and your being green to boot!

5. A Word About Phosphates

A common problem when you first open the pool in the Spring is balancing your pool water chemistry. Every year I see some issue that will ring as a common theme. Last year for example lots of green pools with low PH and Alkaline levels which correlates with the wet, rainy Spring and Summer season we had. This past year was much improved where we actually went swimming early for a change, but I have tested a lot of pools with higher levels of PH and Alkaline at opening time "hmmm" unusual in my experience but we dealt with it by using PH down when appropriate. What I am trying to tell you is that your pool water may behave itself one year and be like a wild child the next all depending upon the outside environment and weather.

Many times I get customers in the store with no chlorine reading at all, first I will test with the computer using my strips but sometimes there may be chlorine there but it is bleaching the pads on the test strip so I will then do a drop test, most times there will be some chlorine when I do this test. However, when there seems to be a *chlorine lock;* that is when there is no free chlorine showing there is something amiss in the water chemistry we *need* to address either by super chlorinating, or testing for other issues such as nitrates or most common in my particular area phosphates.

Now, I was always told that phosphates appeared if you had recently fertilized your lawn, so for years we never tested for phosphates on a regular basis, but there are several ways your pool can become contaminated with fertilizers just being one. Municipalities also use phosphates to clean the water pipes your city water goes through and in our town we have a water tower for one neighborhood which can also be cleaned with phosphate containing materials. Even some chemicals used to take metals out of our pools can contain some phosphates so all these factors add to the list of why your chlorine is being digested too quickly to do its true job of sanitizing your pool. If phosphates are tested for and you have a high level then the fix can be an easy one usually with a treatment of a chemical that removes the phosphates from the pool and you need to follow the instructions of the label to a tee.

As an aside to this, some will say well you can dump half the pool and refill and dilute the phosphates out but let's think this through first. If you think you ended up with the problem because the phosphates are in your water source this will not be the best idea as you will only be repeating the cycle, if you have well water, again, you will need to treat with a sequestering chemical to get the metals out so that's not a good idea either so most times the Phosphate chemical treatment will be the most cost effective route to take.

As I mentioned previously 4-5 years ago we had maybe one or two instances to test for phosphates. Now it has become a persistent problem and I test frequently and find them quite often. Whether they are becoming more prominent by being airborne or through your water source I continue to struggle with treatments. I have had customers who have tried 2-3 different removers and still not solved the problem. I am now finding commercial phosphate removers to be more cost effective and having better results than the residential products for those stubborn cases. Ask your pool professional for their experience in your particular area.

TIP: If you are having hard time holding chlorine in your pool and your other levels are testing fine have your pool store test for phosphates. Most test kits will show up to a certain threshold such as 3000ppm and that's bad, but in all likely hood you could have more parts per million than the test is showing. Start with a minimum dose of phosphate remover but if you still are showing no improvement your levels were probably significantly higher than the test showed and you will need to add dosage.

As a refresher, free available chlorine is that portion of chlorine that is capable of oxidizing contaminants whereas total chlorine residual is the combination of free chlorine and any combined Chloramines. Chloramines are weak cleaners because the chlorine is locked with ammonia and is not available to kill bacteria (chlorine lock). The ammonia comes from human sweat, urine and when there is insufficient chlorine present to combine with all the available ammonia and to oxidize bacteria.

One active swimmer in your pool for one hour produces one quart of sweat per hour. So you may have a test reading total chlorine with no free chlorine and therefore available chlorine is locked.

A myth is that you have plenty of chlorine or high chlorine levels if you smell the odor or have irritated eyes but these are actually signs of chloramines not too much chlorine. In order to neutralize chloramines super chlorination is suggested and there are various methods used with some suggesting up to 8 gallons of liquid chlorine for 20K gallons of pool water circulating the water until the levels read normal. I would suggest no swimming when doing this treatment until your levels become normal again.

I hope you find this book helpful. I always enjoy giving hints and tips on how to be a well-educated home buyer and pool owner. For further information check out my other books on swimming pool ownership!

Pro Pool Girl Book Series includes:

How to Choose a Swimming Pool Contractor

Help! We are Buying a Home with a Swimming Pool: A Guide to Purchasing a Home with a Swimming Pool

Swimming Pool Water Safety: A Guide to Having a Safe Swimming Season

Swimming Pool Equipment: How to Maintain and What Can Be Added

Water Chemistry 101 for your Swimming Pool

Swimming Pool Ownership and Maintenance

All the information in this book is meant to educate the consumer on pool ownership. Please remember that this information is not all inclusive and does not reflect individual geographical situations as to building codes and regulations and this author and her associations do not endorse specific brands and strongly urge owners to consult with their local authorities. The author and or her associations recommend you always contact a local contractor who will be more knowledgeable to your particular situation and area. Although the author and publisher have made every effort to ensure that the information in this book was correct at press time, the author and publisher do not assume and hereby disclaim any liability to any party for any loss, damage, or disruption caused by errors or omissions, whether such errors or omissions result from negligence, accident, or any other cause.

Contact with your comments and suggestions to:

Propoolgirl@prospectpoolsllc.com
www.prospectpoolsllc.com

Made in United States
North Haven, CT
14 September 2024